POEMS FROM AN AVERAGE JOE:

A COLLECTION

9/17/04

To Will,

Enjoy!

— Joe Flechenter

P O E M S

FROM AN AVERAGE JOE:

A COLLECTION

By Joe Fleckenstein

Library of Congress Card Number:
2004092194
ISBN 0-9752677-0-1

First Printing   April 2004

For more information regarding this author & book:
Joe Fleckenstein
President, Average Joe Books
P.O. Box 43480
Baltimore, Maryland 21236-0480
www.averagejoebooks.com

"Joe Knows Writing!"

Printed in the U.S.A. by
Morris Publishing
3212 East Highway 30
Kearney, NE 68847
1-800-650-7888

To the aspiring writers of Baltimore &Beyond:

Persist, Produce, Publish!

Photo Credits

ACKNOWLEDGEMENTS

I am indebted to many people, including:

Alan Lee – without you, none of this would have been
          possible.
Patricia Punt – for helping me to believe in myself.
Marc Stoecker – for introducing me to the world
               of creative thought & writing.

Dave Archer – for making me laugh & keeping my
               spirits high. (ah you tah me)
Chris Fleckenstein – for being there when I needed
               to talk.
My Three Loyal Students From HCC Writing Class --
          You know who you are.
John & Geraldine Fleckenstein – for providing my
          awesome baby photos!

Bernie Lovell – for scanning my photos.
Linda Duvenage – My South African friend.
4 Cute Girls making me look good. Thx Doug/Alex.
Shannon Lord – a special thanks for being mi Diablita.
Author Maxine Kumine, who was my
               unknowing guide.

And the great staff **at Morris Publishing**!

CONTENTS

ONE

TWO

THREE

ONE

MY FAIRY TALE

Reflections

"This was my attempt to write about one of my favorite mythical creatures: *dragons*. Now, I can truly say that I possess my own fairy tale!" –J.T.F.

MY FAIRY TALE

It was a merry jaunt to Camelot,
thirty leagues give or take three,
on horseback would be fleet,
but I traveled on hands and knees,

to warn the elegant Arthur,
of a dragon by the name of Lamb,
don't let his name deceive you,
he dines on armored man.

And if I reached Merlin,
that wizard of wisdom and fame,
or the possessor of ExCalibur,
what was his bloody name?

Because dragons aren't myth,
they are fiercesome and truth,
but they may be bribed or flattered,
by wealthy handsome youth.

This is my role,
in the apocryphal tale,
to combine gold and charisma,
altering the dragon's trail,

away from Camelot and Arthur,
keeping the legends intact,
safe from dragonbreath fire,
it's my duty to make a pact.

The mighty Lamb will not mind,
A nugget of gold or shiny dime,
he will stray from his plan,
because it is written in this rhyme.

My word has always been good,
upholding historical fiction,
it's a pleasure to alter events,
but it creates great friction.

So the apocrypha fades to dust,
Lamb will never meet the Sword,
or sink his teeth into hardened knights,
thanks to my pen.

(Or was it my gold horde?)

TWO SOULS

Reflections

"Thinking back to a young woman who challenged me like no girl had ever inspired me, I actually wrote this inside of an ice-skating rink, furiously shivering as I imagined the two of us engaged in our own private show."—J.T.F.

TWO SOULS

Here we are –
striding on ice,
pressures' on vacation,
the symphony creating,
an atmosphere
of delight;

night approaching,
temperature falling,
except around us,
all alone as February
fades into March,
the sky is dark
but we are the light,
what a sight,
we are.

Maybe the stars are watching,
spying from the distance,
but it really doesn't matter,
because when two souls click,
resistance fades and idle chatter
becomes meaningful,
conversing about dreams,
hopes, and desires,

building the perfect fire,
staying warm on
the winter ice,
dancing and skating,
receiving a private ovation,
from the angels in Heaven.

WOMAN IS GOD

Reflections

"A man must learn to appreciate his wife or girlfriend, and there is no better method than using his God-given tools and talents to his full advantage…"
--J.T.F.

WOMAN IS GOD

My lips are the beginning
of sweet seduction,
light-green eyes melting resistance,
the tongue providing assistance:
to perform passion,
create ecstasy.

A private world,
a capacity
of two,
that will not fade or pass away,
as lips are locked and bodies sway:
the moment frantic, yet endless.

And time was never invented,
because this is love with greater intensity,
higher degree,
than any before.

Continuing until we peak,
then savoring the experience,
as it only makes sense,
to hold the woman of your dreams.

OUR MOMENT TO BLOSSOM

Reflections

"I want to dedicate this work to Shannon –
mi Diablita y novia. And, if I am so
fortunate, mi esposa futura." –J.T.F.

OUR MOMENT TO BLOSSOM

I want to make love to you,
surrounded by leopards and bears,
despite their quizzical stares,
purrs, and growls
we will howl at the moon,
bark at the sun,

For your body most celestial
would make any astronomer blush;
as the rush of blood converges upon
my penis,
Venus and her horny boyfriend Mars
shield themselves from my heavenly juices,
with puffy protective layers,
that Mortals call clouds;

The circle of beasts,
corralling us from Humanity,
impatiently following our example
of *Homosapien* lust,

The rawness of their grunts
as Mother Nature envisioned;
since they are distracted
we escape,

Back to our hotel room,
where we frantically shower,
shave, and shine,

Keeping in mind that our meeting
with the corporate executives
commences,

in a mere five minutes.

MY FIRST APPARITION

Reflections

"My dad and sister, at distinctly separate times, witnessed a female ghost in my childhood home. This prompted me to write my own tale of a mysterious phenomenon." –J.T.F.

MY FIRST APPARITION

When I witnessed my first apparition,
my undershorts, the color of ivory tusks,
were splattered by a mushy, root-beer
colored substance I'd rather not describe
and you'd rather not smell,
but she, and I knew it was a female
because of the soft from of her breasts,
spoke to me in Aramaic, the ancient
language of Jesus, and, surprisingly,
it was purely comprehensible. She told me
that she was a Jew, from an era
long, long, ago, and a resident of Nazarth.
She despised the Romans, and was by trade
the wife of a fisherman, but it was her
next words that deprived me of the use
of my drawers for eternity: *"I was the
sister of Jesus – the one you call, "The
Anointed One – The Christ."*

"Yes, Joseph, son of John," she pronounced
in her guttural tongue. *"You may call me
Mariel. Jesus, little Jessie, he was
four years younger than I. He was a
musical prodigy, my little brother. He perfected
the flute in three lessons; the piano in four.
He was fluent in the languages of Greek,
Hebrew, and that of the Ethiopian. He was as
fleet as an African hunter. He counseled
the Visitors with his wisdom and mysticism;
He used his healing touch to repair their
starship's reactors and tractor rays."*

22

"What!!" I suddenly began to doubt the
ludicrous words of the apparition.
"There were no spaceships in The Bible!
Jesus didn't play any instruments. How dare
you blaspheme and make light of the
humanity and life of my Savior! You should be
ashamed of yourself!"

The apparition chuckled; it seemed that Mariel
had anticipated my harsh reaction and sudden outburst.
*"Joseph, your Gospels, as lovely as they are,
say nothing of Jessie's early years –
and, why should they? My brother was a
jet-setter from the age of twelve until
twenty-six, two millennia before jumbo airliners
were invented. He logged approximately
56,700 miles; from India to Siam; Peru to Mexico.
He even visited the natives of your Chesapeake Bay –
for three months, on the cusp of His eighteenth
birthday. The Visitors taught him culture
and science; Jessie taught them compassion
and peace."*

*"But, Jessie never left your planet, and as He,
Mother, Father, and James waved goodbye
to the Visitors the day after His 31st year,
His ministry as you knew it formally began."*

*"Remember my Brother always, Joseph, for
He loves you dearly. Loves you more than you
could ever fathom."*

Then she vanished. Yet, I was alive, and into
song I burst, *"Amazing Grace, how sweet
the sound..."*

* *"Amazing Grace"* was composed by John Newton,
c. 1765*

TIME IN THREE QUARTERS

Reflections

"The hands of a grandfather clock are visually stimulating, unlike the sterile coldness of a modern digital timepiece. It is with this image that love and time collide." –J.T.F.

TIME IN THREE QUARTERS

My heart is three-quarters,
but fifteen minutes shy,
one-fourth still missing,
realization won't deny,

For you are the package,
I would love to unveil,
so calm and quite gentle,
but I yearn for a gale,

Not a stormy disposition,
or a violent rain,
but a saucy undercurrent,
cutting against the grain,

Who understands the many worlds,
in which I call home,
who tolerates the earthiness,
of a mind obliged to roam,

As the clock strikes its hour,
I humbly look upon you,
for forty-five we lived together,
then another fills my view.

TO LEEZA

Reflections

"An expression of lust and passion; little
more need be said…" –J.T.F.

TO LEEZA

No longer do I heed the warnings
  of Catholic wisdom,
I want to cuddle with you
  on the coldest of mornings,
start the fire in the afternoon,
and release my tension in the evening:
pouring hot liquid into a dark cavern,
igniting the lava that flows so free
erupting under moonlit sky,
then recharging for midnight penetration
adding fuel to free-flowing fluids;
boiling juices and intense heat
propelling bodies beyond the stars
into that new realm
seldom seen on our stifled planet,
where mind and body
soul and spirit
are but a single entity;
an enlightened state
beyond the experience of a priest
without common frame of reference,
and as dawn approaches
we are receptive of the Sun,
flesh covering flesh,
evolving into one.

RAMBLINGS OF AN UNIMAGINATIVE WRITER

Reflections

"Is my imagination really that poor? You decide!" –J.T.F.

RAMBLINGS OF AN UNIMAGINATIVE WRITER

The slithering Serpent delivered a Sermon,
suggestive of slimy intrigue,
directed at Adam and Eve,

Fruitful gain the topic of discussion,
daring and deceiving,
the Serpent never retreating,
for Unholy Words sound so sweet.

How does one beat temptation,
avoid moral decay,
they knew God's way
was the answer,

But pride turned the tide,
desecrating a bond
between Creator and Man,

The Lord shuttering in Wrath,
Appalled by their decision,
Hence a division
as sin entered the fold.

Though we are bold and brave
we cannot cleanse unclean souls,
for that was the task of a Warrior

who was more than just a Courier,
grabbing the Serpent by the throat,
forcing Him to choke,
giving back those who embraced
the Sermon,

Granting an avenue of escape
through sacrifice and denial,
ultimately placed on trial
but risen in victory:

THE JOLTIN' JEW,
THE PALESTINE PRIZE,
FROM DEATH TO ALIVE,
AT 5'10" AND 160 LBS,
IN THE BLOODY TRUNKS,
JESUS OF NAZARETH!!!

RESIDUAL MEMORY

Reflections

"I wont' say anything about this one –
you'll have to draw your own
conclusions." –J.T.F.

RESIDUAL MEMORY

Remembering her story,
Infatuation,
on a clear summer's day
when the world was alright.

Recalling the details,
Anticipating,
the love that was felt
but the gain that was lost.

Responding with passion,
Overreacting,
emotions cloud vision
as the saga unfolds.

Repressing her feelings,
A Compensation,
to react with balance
because folly is fool.

Retaining the fragments,
As endless dwelling
does harm to the soul,
so it's time to let go.

PREOCCUPIED

Reflections

"The subject matter of this poem bothered and harassed me for years; then again, it is the experience of the entire male gender from planet Earth!"
–J.T.F.

PREOCCUPIED

There is but one delay in life,
something men cannot avoid,
toying with our thoughts,
entrenched upon the mind,
although shoved behind
the daily needs of today.

It cannot be ignored
until the void is filled,
as we build up our defenses
we are overtaken by
one of them:
the sight, the smell,
hair tossed about by a gentle breeze,
perhaps it is Nature's tease,

But she looks so lovely,
that she is a permanent fixture,
a wicked memory.

Can I have her –
a question that cannot be answered by science,
only self-esteem and kindness
can get you across that bridge,
with the help of some wit and an open mind,
you may find,
an occupant for the void, and a woman to enjoy.

COMMA LITTLE BIT CLOSER

Reflections

"Contact me on my website or catch me at a book-signing, and I'll explain this one to you!" –J.T.F.

COMMA LITTLE BIT CLOSER

Happiness is being a comma,
pausing here and there,
adding spice to any genre,
taking a moment to reflect
and longing for a way,
to keep sloppy, neglectful,
careless thought away:

> *An ode to Shatner –*
> *that Master of Pause,*
> *or any artist with the balls,*
> *to take a dramatic stand.*

Include me
in your composition,
I am the transition,
a barrier to be broken,
but an obstacle none-the-less;
What a mess
if I didn't exist,
could you risk it without me,
and really pull it off?

I think not,
the page that is bare of my mark,
is like a runner in the dark,
missing direction,
never staying the course,
resigning in disgrace.

> *But Shatner knows his place:*
> *the embodiment of drama,*
> *like a father to the comma,*
> *and a hero to the nation.*

DISSECTING THE GAME

Reflections

"One of my fantasies is to become a Chess Master, but my seven-year-old niece kicks my butt at this game (and at Checkers, too!) This is my tribute to man over machine." –J.T.F.

DISSECTING THE GAME

The IBM layoff hurt many,
but not Kasparov
(Garry to his friends,)
the liberator of oppression,
a modern-day cosmonaut
who plots
thirty-two moves per second;
as Russians beckon
their Countryman on
in the war against capitalism,
greed and machinery,
even the IBM disenfranchised
have a destiny:

Defeat *Deep Blue,*
and make headline news,
disperse your pawns as
we do Marines,
into crisis centers,
but this time with the
means of support,
preferably knights, bishops
and rooks,
get your nose out of the books,
study time is gone,
time to defeat
the Evil One.

Man versus his own creation;
an elated joy as Kasparov
does not go soft
on his opponent,
utilizing a
lifetime of components,
inching toward victory,
one move at a time.

Deep Blue is worthy,
but Kasparov
sees through its strategies,
the Russian preparing
a eulogy
for his enemy;

As technology reared its
ugly head and gave
us all a scare,
Garry was there,
cheered by the
unemployed non-descript
spectators,
and a great Bear.

Deep Blue II will get revenge;
as the wealthy avenge
the dismal showing of their latest software,
Kasparov just stares,
then smiles as he takes on the challenge,
trying to keep balance,
and harmony,
in check.

GLOBAL IDOLS

Reflections

"This is my salute to the powerful icons of Rock 'n Roll." –J.T.F.

GLOBAL IDOLS

Some of my idols are alive and well,
while many have passed through the gates of Heaven,
still others struggle through a personal Hell,
a few possess incomes in the digit of seven.

Robert Plant and Jimmy Page,
the stars of a zep named Led,
a mystical sound that sweetens with age,
but only three as one is dead.

When Hell froze over five men survived,
California harmony and Southern sound,
American fliers soaring open skies,
destined for greatness when pettiness drowned.

Then four masked men jumped the gate,
rocking Detroit proving they were the best,
a starchild demon chased a cat who was spaced,
the critics said no but the audience screamed yes!

But the absolute best invaded the USA,
when our nation struck its lowest point,
just take a stroll down Penny Lane,
pick up your Hofner and roll a joint.

Well, drugs never solved anything,
but global idols who could sway world opinion,
from Vietnam to ethnic cleansing,
have opened doors to a new dominion.

(And made many a girl wet.)

TWO

THE FREEDOM OF LOVE

Reflections

"I almost lost this poem, immediately after its' conception. Thank God it was recovered! One of the most simple but sincere works I have ever penned." –J.T.F.

THE FREEDOM OF LOVE

I want to lift you up
into my cloud,
my haven, my home,
nestled among friends,
above the birds and the rain,
where we abstain from war,
and converse with gods...

Picking berries and sipping wine,
unaware of time,
and the barriers of man
for paradise belongs to dreamers,
my vision is clear,
my mind open,
my soul
cleansed...

Thanks to you,
immortal lady,
my partner in life,
and everafter.

DRAGONSONG

Reflections

"This was actually intended as a song, for young children. My original inspiration was, *'The Yellow Submarine,'* by The Beatles." –J.T.F.

DRAGONSONG

Lonely dragon, it'll be alright,
legend of terror, as you stalk the night,
you work real hard, you are king of the sky,
you live by a code, that is noble and high.

Flames of fire, leap out of your mouth,
your angry roar, turns man into mouse,
you try so hard, to be firm yet fair,
the kingdom you rule, is one we must share.

Dragonsong, Dragonsong,
everyone cries the Dragonsong,
the rich and the poor, the weak and the strong,
everyone cries the Dragonsong,
everyone cries the Dragonsong.

Lonely dragon, don't despair,
the subjects you rule – hawk, eagle, and bear,
just give them a chance, and they'll come around,
send out your love, and they'll flock to the sound…

Of your Dragonsong, Dragonsong,
everyone cries the Dragonsong,
the rich and the poor, the weak and the strong,
everyone cries the Dragonsong,
yeah, everyone cries the Dragonsong.

LORENA

Reflections

"I love strong women, fully capable of taking on the world. *'Lorena'* is such a heroine, embroiled in the most difficult of circumstances." –J.T.F.

LORENA

From the Rappahannock to the Susquehanna,
in every pond between,
delved a spy whose allegiance
favored the Confederacy,

An angelic seductress,
with a sharpshooter's stare,
she could waltz and foxtrot,
outrun a swift deer,

Her instincts predatory,
her intelligence keen,
she infiltrated the Federals
shooting a bullet into the spleen,

Of a Northern assassin,
intent on collapsing
the Infamous Southern Firm,
of Davis/Lee/Jackson,

Then licking pouty lips,
flashing lightning eyes,
pulling skyward her gown,
exposing juicy thighs,

She advanced upon her lover,
a Union boy from Maryland,
whose heart began to flutter,
loyalty waver,

Then falter and crumble
as she whispered Rebellious secrets
into his ears,
then silenced him with kisses,
caresses and tears,

For she had done her duty,
clear conscience without shame,
even though the South,
would receive all the blame,

The Carpetbagger lover,
she converted that night,
promised her a Union,
matrimonial without fight,

…and time expended itself…

Today she's retired,
he's an ex-Yankee,
they grow old in a farmhouse,
indulging in panky
(hanky, that is,)
and lovin' every minute of one another.

SOCIAL GRACES

Reflections

"It is vital that we never forget the crimes of brutal regimes, past and present." – J.T.F.

SOCIAL GRACES

Fluent and flawless
smooth and swanlike
the prisoners danced
waltzed to the tempo

The synchronized beat
very light on their feet
never stepping on toes
couples in motion

Lovers and friends
Jews and Gentiles
in ballroom elegance
turning as one

And then a dirge that final hour,
the music ended in the shower.

BARNYARD REVENGE

Reflections

"Ceciltucky is a code word for, *'Cecil County,'* a traditionally rural county located in northeastern Maryland." –J.T.F.

BARNYARD REVENGE

Remember the time –
grass-fed cattle grazing lazily
on the hard, stiff straw
clumped along that bump,
inside the crack of your ass.

Your face was beautiful –
angelic yet unusual,
caked with gooey manure,
a muddy stain on a dirt floor,
your mouth filled with dingleberries.

And the sheep and the pigs
gnawing on your ribs,
looking for feed from a body of flesh,
at least if you were John Tesh
you could frighten them with a concert.

But you were a radio personality,
and on your stomach you lay,
a discarded jock with a severed cock,
trying to convert the farmers to a format of rock;
but the constituents of country

Like most of Ceciltucky
made an example of you,
and now the barnyard animals
listen to old-school bluegrass,
with an oink and a moo.

A HUMBLED MAN

Reflections

"My only observation is that some people just don't learn…" –J.T.F.

A HUMBLED MAN

I.   I can't catch my breath,
I'm running out of life and
slipping away,
into the cradle,
rocked to sleep by gentle lullabies,
feasting on mother's bosom,
although I prefer my wife,
the challenge of bringing her to
sexual climax, washing her
breasts with my tantalizing tongue,

II.   Fantasizing about the love we used to
make,
and the cookies she would bake,
after the children went to bed.

III.   I am led to another room,
cavernous and cold,
yet stirred by a sense of peace,
complete with altar and candles,
prayer book and priest,
using the Confessional to clear my
conscience,
finding new life as sins are told,
and forgiven.

IV.   But what remains hidden is that one sin,
the one that turns eight hours of sleep into
two,
as I think of you, I dwell on my broken
relationship with God, and the
secret that is hidden.

V.   I didn't want to ruin our challenge,
the prospect of twenty glorious years together,
but along came Heather, and life became
better…

VI.   …well, except for the sex,
it was tedious and tiring,
hiding the truth from you – my wife,
my partner in life
and mother of my children.

VII.   I'm saying goodbye to mother's bosom,
the stuffed animals and baby toys,
leaving the cradle for a shot at redemption,
please make an exception and forgive me,
hear my plea,
give me life and drop the lawsuit,
adultery's wrong and I want you.

But then there's Stacey…

PICNIC

Reflections

"I have very little sympathy for the greedy and self-centered of this world." –J.T.F.

PICNIC

Insects drive me crazy;
how can one picnic with a host
of ants, bees, and flies,
competing for the sustenance
that keeps me alive.
I know other ants, bees, and
flies,
who walk upright with
opposable thumbs,
numb to the needs of the world;
only caring about their next meal,
swarming to funerals and family
disasters,
fighting to inherit heirlooms that really mattered
to the former owner,
ambitious and greedy for that free ride,

But my sister and me look them straight
in the eye,
pull out our swatters and insect repellant,
fighting the hosts with a Hell-Bent
spirit that refuses to compromise
with the leeches and insects the deceased despised,

Because I want to picnic with those who really cared,
for the one who was lost, and the memories we'd
shared.

MESSAGE

Reflections

"Regardless of your religion or belief system, you would be wise to consider the unshakable wisdom from this unique messenger." –J.T.F.

MESSAGE

Out of the womb, and into the room,
a beautiful Child was born that day,
to frolic and play His full-time career,
could only talk by crying those tears.

While mommy and daddy refrained from their beer,
coolers of wine, and whiskey so fine,
the Lad grew –
a carpenter's Son,
always having fun,
assisting the peasants with
His handyman's touch,
gentle and wise,
never saying too much…

…until that day when He had His calling;
because He knew in His heart that
the Jews were falling,
into a trap – away from the Word,
He wanted to preach,
teach and praise,
His Father in Heaven,
for granting this day.

So He broke
uncharted ground,
espousing a message
that most found
to be Satanic,
or just mere talk,
while most balked
at the tool-time Rebel,
a crowd did join –

--most dressed
in little more than loins,
they went on tour,
the Young Man
addressing

every facet
of life,
from the humble beggar,
to the soldiers of might,
providing answers
to the obvious questions,
making God number one,
and religion old-fashioned:

All good things
must come to an end,
but as emperors reign
and evil widens,
there is little room
from crying,
because the carpenter's Son
put on

one heck of a show,
and we should know,
that nothing
can stop us now.

THE DATE THAT NEVER WAS

Reflections

"The story of a mock date gone good –
and bad." –J.T.F.

THE DATE THAT NEVER WAS

The Inquisition followed
her to work,
a jealous boyfriend with
impeccable taste, a
rational mind and
no time to waste,

Makes an advance,
then drifts out of sight,
shadow to shadow,
staying out of the light.

The girlfriend preparing
to set-up a date,
with a brilliant young man
dressed casual but cool;
the boyfriend drools,
drips and boils
with anger,
and hatred for
the lucky fellow.

The two say hello,
then farewell to work,
for a friendly evening
of dinner and dance,
minus romance,

Because the two only
had conversation
in mind,
but hatred is blind
to simple truths,

as the Inquisition loops
the rope around his neck,
what began as a trek
to follow his beloved,

became a disgusting trial
of paranoia
versus trust,
as the dust
settles over
the defunct lover,
the other two smother
each other with kindness,
but never a kiss,
because it wasn't a tryst,
just the date that never was.

JUDAS' OTHER PLAN

Reflections

"Sometimes the Devil works in mysterious ways." –J.T.F.

JUDAS' OTHER PLAN

Jesus on acid would be the coup de grace,
loosening up for His sermon,
babbling and blurting
out unseen wisdom
and undiscovered truths,
suddenly finding His youth,
expanding the Kingdom,
making His Father sigh

…because Jesus was high,
and finally on the level
of the vagabond beggar
on an all-night bender,
beyond comprehension or recall,
trying to explain it all
to the crowd of fifty-five
scribes, fishermen, and tax collectors.

But

Jesus ran from His creditors,
and flying high He was tried
and found guilty for His teachings,
so they threw Him on a cross,
as He prayed to His Boss
he begged for more acid,
as He did
the world was at a loss

Because Satan threw a 'trip' colossal,
disrupting salvation,
spoiling God's vacation,
in the guise of a trusted apostle.

RACIST HOAX

Reflections

"Why can't we just get *past* this inherent evil known as racism? We weren't born with this contaminant, were we?" –J.T.F.

RACIST HOAX

Black Power is darkness,
White Power a cloak
to cover-up hatred,
to make good people choke,
gag and spit as we live

       Together

in this game of struggle,
if only we could snuggle
in the bosom of our Mother,
secure and nurtured,
never tempted by wrong,
rejoicing in song,
taking life one step further
than this racist hoax.

LUMP

Reflections

"This one always makes me smile. I hope that it has a positive effect on you!" – J.T.F.

LUMP

I've got a lump on the middle of my rump,
a breathtaking calcium deposit,
yet my back is not humped,
my spine ramrod straight,

Walking with the gait of a soldier
marching in a victory parade,
in celebration of God and country,
my lump providing the needed shade,

And further down the line,
as sixty rolled into seventy,
and Social Security hurt my vanity
my lump never subsided,
never grayed or wrinkled,
always a reminder,
better than a freckle or pimple,

Keeping life simple,
romantic and practical,
a permanent interest-bearing investment,
a rent-free resident,
a hump that is not a stump,
bearing life and character,

Blessed by God
        not cursed by Satan,
time to stop the hating;
        frigid minds that will not thaw,
unlike babies who only crawl,
        only see death,
where I see beauty – and life.

THREE

THE SERVER BEING SERVED

Reflections

"Would you attend a dinner party thrown by Adolf Hitler? Well, someone apparently did…"—J.T.F.

Note: 'Zeroes' were a type of popular World War II fighter-plane used by the Japanese against the Allies.

THE SERVER BEING SERVED

Hitler invited Satan to dinner, the winter of '39, luring the fiery Demon with recipes of crimes against humanity, while portraying himself as Fuhrer, leader, and hero; as Japanese Zeroes flew Pacific skies and brought horror to Pacific nations, Adolf concocted a scheme even more grand: Blame the Jews and evoke a reign of terror; the fairer ones' skin the healthier in Nazi social clubs – avoid the pubs graced by the Torah, only frequent those displaying a Swastika. No dietary restrictions, limitations, or calculations of caloric intake; this recipe would shake the foundations of Man and the Kingdom of God, only needing the Devil's approval.

Satan's pyrogenic personality began to shine. *"Young Adolf, in five years time you conquer Europe and England, then stab Russia from behind. Capture Stalin and drink his blood, eat his brains and roll in the mud, until covered from head to toe in earthy goo. Obey me, and you'll never lose."*

Hitler, disgusted with his guest, rebuked, *"You force me to puke. I am no animal, and certainly not a cannibal. Why must you alter my recipe? Here, calm your nerves with some hot tea."*

Satan drew a sulphuric sigh, lit a cigar and adjusted his tie. *"With you I shall never again dine. And in six years you will be mine. Go ahead and burn your Jews. I'd rather dine on a monster like you."*

MEDIEVAL TALES

Reflections

"This is almost a darker version of my earlier poem, *'My Fairy Tale.'* Remember, vampires never drink…wine."—J.T.F.

MEDIEVAL TALES

I. Medieval tales that frightened peasants,
    horrified soldiers and haunted kings,
    were not the dreams of fiction
    but the reality of fact,
    armored men ready to attack
    fell prey to a thoughtful suggestion,
    that led to a lifetime
    of addiction.

II. Medieval myths did not
    fade into dreams,
    as rifles replaced weapons of steel,
    vampiric hordes searched their next meal,
    thirsty for blood only humans could offer,
    the touch of a female,
    always much softer,

III. Than an arrogant lawyer or
    a streetwalking hustler,
    unblemished flesh so ripe for the take;
    the vampires readying for the rape
    of an innocent schoolgirl,
    only seventeen,

IV. Preparing for the Sisterhood
    at the local parish,
    wearing a Cross,
    keeping the nightmarish
    demons away,
    so that she may pray
    to her Father Almighty.

V. But the men known as the Nosferatu,
     wise to the ways of the Virgin,
     operated with the grace of a surgeon,
     liberating her from mortality,
     granting her strength and vitality.

VI. Now she lives as they do,
     vulnerable by day,
     by night a bloodsucking ghoul,
     hiding from Christians,
     Crucifixes and light,
     giving birth to legends,
     perfecting her bite!!

ESCAPE

Reflections

"I wrote this ditty for a college literature course. It wasn't good enough for my professor, but that is *his* loss and *our* gain!"—J.T.F.

ESCAPE

When a hectic world brings you down,
exhaustion fills the mind,
the ship you sail run aground,
your helmsman half-blind.

When a hectic world cares no more,
offers no remorse,
the vessel's direction mistaken,
your navigator off-course.

When a hectic world encompasses,
reveals its dirty tricks,
the crew stricken with Scurvy,
your physician cannot fix.

> But remember Sweet Delilah,
> that child of Nature Fair,
> she was the only on-board,
> with sweet golden-brown hair.
>
> And her sister Angelisa,
> radiant as a star,
> point the compass her direction,
> you will go very far.

Nature always sends it finest,
when man is at his worst,
the Atlantic has a Divineness,
that will quench a man's thirst.

When a hectic world frightens you,
devours your ambition,
embrace the sea like a woman,
employ an old tradition.

GRANDDAD

Reflections

"Everyone in America should observe Veteran's Day. There is so much that we can learn from those who have fought in our country's armed conflicts." –J.T.F.

GRANDDAD

Granddad stifled me with claustrophobic conversation,
tales of gaudy masks and chloric gas,
episodes of influenza that would not pass,
no opportunity for contemplation;
        a duty reserved for others
        whose sons and brothers
        worked on Wall Street,
        or bedded the wives
        of front-line fodder.

Yet granddad spoke with clarity,
dignity and temperament,
I may have detected a trace of sadness,
but certainly not nostalgia --
no yearning for the good ole days;

Granddad in rare form,
his face a reflection
        of the mood of the day,
an oral historian,
without journal or photograph –
for physical reminders
        often poison the mind,
        suffocate the Spirit,

How does one get to that Higher Plane,
to escape horrors
rationality won't erase,
like locking oneself in a safe,
discarding the combination…

But granddad resides on Earth,
he copes better than most,
perhaps by telling his tale,
holding my hand,

He takes a personal stand on justice;
such a gracious host,
not reading from Bible or tome,
an alternative form of knowledge,
of wisdom, only two miles from home.

SANIQUARIUM

Reflections

"I admit it…this poem is **weird!** Read it carefully, though. Enjoy!!" – J.T.F.

SANIQUARIUM

Aunt Ginny was a talker,
Cousin Nel a virgin,
Uncle Raymond spent ten years
to become a licensed surgeon.

My grandpa used a walker,
Molly had double chins,
father repressed his feelings
while tilling soil in the gardens.

I am just a fish.

The butler prepared dinner,
our maid stole jewelry,
the nanny cared for children
while tending to her brewery.

Grandma's priest was a sinner,
the nun dwelt in misery,
Deacon Ted cared for the flock
but not for mother's miffery.

I am just a fish:
      Swimming in my tank,
      how the water stank,
      never being fed,
      trapped in my bed.

All the hustle and bustle,
of a busy household,
everyone with an agenda,
how my room is getting cold!

Arrogance flexed its muscle,
their negligence was bold,
an outcast in my own house,
it is the truth that you are told.

You are just a fish:
> Alone without rank,
> no money in the bank,
> when loved ones have fled,
> leaving you for dead.

SET A PATH

Reflections

"This poem is my tribute to the Average Jills and Joes of the world. People who make an honest living, and fight for *common-sense* causes." –J.T.F.

SET A PATH

I.   Your protest carries on
through the night,
as neighbors try to sleep,
sound begins to cease,
you cry out, *"Save the geese,
the whales, the sheep,"*
academic nonsense I try
to avoid,
but your pretty little banner
states the theme of your cause,
addressing issues most do not
pause to contemplate,

II.   Which is great,
because as you waste your youth
on trivial adventures,
acculturating the alternative and
accepting no other,
my lifestyle is normal and clean,
I can safely categorize you
into a minority of freaks,
breaking trends and building anew,
wandering through life with
the mindset of a generation,
that now regards you as
ridiculous and absurd –
I've heard that you're going
out of style.

III.   As you close on thirty,
attend your rallies,
my wife Sally opens her yearbook,
take a look –
you haven't changed in over ten years;

IV.   While the rest of us pursue
goals that are clear,
focusing on the spouse and the kids,
balancing work and school
with leisure time,
fighting the real issues,
like traffic and crime,
there you debate,
about the health of a lake,
confronting the issues of your day!

V.   Use your talents for society's sake,
please set a path,
do not stray,
because very soon blonde becomes gray.

MANICURE, ANYONE?

Reflections

"I know…I know…yes, I am guilty of biting my nails! It is disgusting, sure, but I have an excuse. You see, it's not really me doing the biting…" --J.T.F.

MANICURE, ANYONE?

Once a week, during my
hours of sleep, I am visited
by a Creature Nocturnal,
eating the sheep I've been dreaming,
devouring the meat, red from bleeding,

Then without peep, cackle, or
hiss, opening lips that
never kiss, restraining drool
and saliva while licking jagged
tools – thirty-two of them, the
rotted black teeth like unbrushed
utensils,

this Monster nesting inside my
walls nibbles and munches on
the nails of my claws – for
personal pleasure or nourishment
I really don't know –
curiously avoiding my toes,

Who He is, and why He
tortures me, I cannot gather,

for my nails are clearly bitten, of
that there can be no doubt;
on Saturdays my girlfriend
visits, whining with a pout,
*"Joe! Stop biting your nails! That's
disgusting! Get a pair of clippers!"*

My reaction is always swift
and stern,
"At least I don't bite my toenails!"

I rebuke, offended that she should
intrude, so much, *every weekend,*
on my personal hygiene,

when in reality I knew the truth. *If*
only I could capture Him, Her, or
It – That Little Shit – er, Piece of
Excrement, I mean,
and drive Him from my walls,
my house,

But, the Louse in question
won't take a hint --
won't loosen His hold,
won't quit His teething –
until I learn to take

control of my actions. Yes! *You
heard me!* If I would simply enjoy
the moment, let the future shape
itself, I wouldn't gnaw my nails.
There's no Night Goblin chewing
my cuticles. Of course not!

It's me! It was *me* all along. I
just wanna know…Why am
I so damned insecure?

PRAY FOR OUR CLERGY

Reflections

"I believe with all of my heart that the overwhelming majority of priests, ministers, and evangelists are dedicated, sincere, and morally responsible individuals. But, what to do when one encounters a religious leader with less than noble values and ethics?" --J.T.F.

PRAY FOR OUR CLERGY

Picture a man with Southern charm,
a gentle charisma that the masses adore,
prevailing in wisdom –keeping others from harm,
greeting the people as they come to his door.

Follow that man and you will be like me,
a nervous young pastor who is going gray,
for Original Sin can strike very deep,
when even the Blessed are turning away,

into a Blackness – covered by robes,
Bibles, and Crosses to spread The Word;
but the message of love and the lessons of Job,
get mixed reviews in this Demon Church.

Pray for a man who once had a calling,
to a selfless life of fruitful gain,
and think about me when your world is falling,
how can I help you when I'm full of pain?

THE GIG (A DUET)

Reflections

"Conversations with God are often
enlightening, but the Almighty *has* a sense
of humour! I'm quite convinced of it."
–J.T.F.

THE GIG (A DUET)

MAN: I was given a task last night,
             gotta entertain God,
             choose between guitar and sax,
             whichever I select I'll reply via fax.
                   So
             I pulled out my six-string,
             strummed away to Crosby, Stills, and Nash,
             God seemed to like it and I was pleased,
             "Dear Lord…just pay me in cash!"

GOD: *"Oh my Child…I can't do that,*
             Money will just bring you down,
             I've got a gift that'll never go away,
             My Child you were lost…now you're found."

MAN: "Now wait a minute," I replied with a grin,
             "I work for money, don't pay me and You sin.
             I expected more…Father Almighty,
             Don't work for free…damn, You are flighty."

GOD: *"Silence…my ungrateful Child!*
             You've got a gift and a wonderful smile.
             Use your talents, and work for me,
             That might mean a few gigs come free."

MAN: "Wait…You live in Heaven,
             I live in Cleveland,
             I'm just trying to earn a living.
             I've got a wife and kids to support,
             What You propose will leave me cash short."

GOD: *"Just have faith, my talented Man,*
      Like your Mother, for you I have a plan,
      To bring My Kingdom into
      the hearts of Others,
      Expand My pool of Sisters and Brothers."

AND THE MAN PONDERED GOD'S WISDOM

AND PONDERED

AND PONDERED

(HE WAS STUBBORN, YOU SEE)

THEN, FINALLY...

MAN: Upon reflection, the Big Guy was right,
      for His Kingdom is open all night,
      the gigs will come...the cash will flow,
      welcome to...The World's Greatest Show!!

33

Reflections

"This was the first poem that I ever wrote. I wrote it inside of a McDonald's, before attending a college course in New Testament Theology that evening. This poem captures Jesus' opinion of Mankind – past and present." --J.T.F.

33

At the ripe old age of 33,
I was put to death – one of three,
some days later I came back with a smile,
bewildering my followers – innocent and shy.

Many years later I hear my name,
the cries of soldiers dying in vain,
I shed tears as I stare at their blood,
innocent fools as they fall in the mud.

Then people say that I'm coming again,
to rescue Humanity from torment and pain,
but I laugh as I hear the choirs sing,
over 2000 years -- haven't learned a thing.

Maybe someday we'll all be together,
we'll dance eternal to the songs of shepherds,
for now, though, I'll just be content,
to wait for a time when Man will repent.

ROYAL DROPPINGS

.

Reflections

"You will have an entirely new respect for the raw talents of the King's Court Jester upon your reading of this soon-to-be classic masterpiece!" –J.T.F.

ROYAL DROPPINGS

A defecation picker-upper,
a sanitation engineer,
doubling as palace minstrel
bringing nobles to tears,
with a comic act and a
        dog named Spot,
a broom and a pan and a mop,
always in the company of kings,
        yet his only possession a cot.

But how can one sleep when royalty gets pissed,
        modern plumbing still centuries away,
        his lips are moist yet never kissed,
        his hair with a speck of gray,

from a stressful life of
        feces and comedy,
a Deadly Combination –
        but not even minimum wage,
            Spot doesn't even have a cage!

And nobles never act their age,
        after-hours, behind closed doors,
grabbing the bosoms of wenches and ladies,
sloppy slander slobbered from shameless mouths,
        we feel pity for the minstrel,

yet he is the cause of his own misfortune:
the comedy, the flowing ale, half of the nobles
        missing the pale,
urine stains place a strain on the knees and back,
        cleaning the mess,
        but we digress!

For Palace Minstrel hyphen Janitor is
the perfect position:
        a rival king's spy placed in the middle
        of merriment,
while hands clean and mouth sings,
eyes and ears spot everything,
tongues go free when whiskey is loose,
such a deadly juice;
        so he dances and sings,
        donning the white stockings,
        all in the hopes
        of catching Royal Droppings!

PUCKER UP

Reflections

"You've reached the end –
congratulations! Visit my website and
share your thoughts and comments. I
leave you with a history of one of my
favorite pastimes – and it isn't baseball!
Muchas gracias y hasta luego, amigo!"
--J.T.F.

PUCKER UP

The Goddess of Love, and the King of the Earth,
made sweet love, in no time gave birth
to a Maiden of Splendour, with a beauty so fair,
no mere Mortal was she, as she danced on the air.

As pure as snow, she could melt your heart,
until she was kissed under the Mistletoe,
by a Frenchman from Nice, who could kiss
with such passion,
that his *kiss* became famous, after a fashion.

Armed with the knowledge of her newfound pucker,
this Maiden of Heaven began to sucker
in handsome young men, almost of age, and
kissed with such passion, using her tongue as bait.

Showering adolescents with the secrets of her Kiss,
the young men evangelized and spread the myth
to any girl who was daring and curious,
dispelling rumours, making foreplay glorious.

But was it really their fault
they engaged in oral pleasures;
after being kissed by a Maiden
it was time for new measures.

This is one of many versions
of the Kiss called *French,*
an exercise in lust,
started by a Maiden,
and a gigolo from Nice,
who in the interest of peace,

Swept a Lady off her feet --
granting the lads a present,
with which they are never hesitant.

ABOUT THE AUTHOR

A little taller and heavier than the above picture, the Joe
Fleckenstein of today dreams that his life revolved
around eating, sleeping, and taking care of business,
with a little children's television sprinkled in for good
measure, but the demands of a real-world job have
temporarily stifled this fantasy. A native of Bel Air,
Maryland, he currently resides a few miles outside of
Baltimore, where he grows and expands his promising
writing empire. Friendly and humble, he is the boy-
next-door, who seeks fulfillment in life by spending as
much time as possible with his girlfriend, childhood
pals, and family. *Poems From An Average Joe: A
Collection* is his first book – but there will be more!

FOR MORE INFORMATION

CHECK OUT MY WEBSITE AT:

www.averagejoebooks.com

My website features:

- Periodic drawings for gift cards to national bookstore chains, exclusive only to purchasers of this book

- An opportunity for you, the reader, to provide your own review of this book, and an outlet to express your comments, opinions, and feedback

- The latest updates on my personal appearances, lectures, and book-signings.

- An opportunity to order additional copies of this book.

To order additional copies of this book:

- Send your name and mailing address, along with a check or money order payable to: *Average Joe Books (or) Joseph Fleckenstein* *P.O. Box 43480* *Baltimore, MD 21236-0480* **Send $12.00 plus $3.00 shipping/handle/tax.** You will receive your order within 2 to 4 business days.

- Or, visit my website and order securely by major credit card. Same charges and delivery apply. See website for more details!